What mattersmost of All

School is about More than ABCs

SMART ADVICE FROM TEACHER TO PARENT

Heather S. Agee and Marie E. Miller

Copyright © 2017 by NOW SC Press

All rights reserved. No part of this publication may be reproduced, distributed, or transmitted in any form or by any means, including photocopying, recording, or other electronic or mechanical methods, without the prior written permission of the publisher, except in the case of brief quotations embodied in critical reviews and certain other noncommercial uses permitted by copyright law. For permission requests, write to the publisher, addressed "Attention: Permissions Coordinator," via the website below.

1.888.5069-NOW

www.nowscpress.com

@nowscpress

Ordering Information:

Quantity sales. Special discounts are available on quantity purchases by corporations, associations, and others. For details, contact the publisher at the address above.

Orders by U.S. trade bookstores and wholesalers. Please contact: NOW SC Press: Tel: (888) 5069-NOW or visit www.nowscpress.com.

Printed in the United States of America

First Printing, 2017

ISBN: 978-0-9987391-7-5

Heather

I dedicate this book to my husband, Jeff, and my children, Tilden and Charlotte, for their funny, practical encouragement along the way. I'm thankful for the support of my sister, Allison, who is always a giver of wisdom and insight. I would also like to thank my parents for their love and care.

Marie

I would like to dedicate this book to my parents, who always provided a loving and caring home. I'm also grateful for my dearest friend Steph; the consummate cheerleader in my life. And also to my pride and joy, my two little furry friends, my cats: Sophie and Pinky.

Contents

Chapter One
False Ideas We Believe 1

Chapter Two
Your Presence is Powerful 13

Chapter Three
Developing a Positive Mindset 25

Chapter Four
Maintaining the Joy in Perseverance 37

Chapter Five
Helping Your Child Develop Good Peer-to-Peer Relationships 49

Chapter Six
No Kid is Perfect... 65

Chapter Seven
Communication is a Two-Way Effort 73

Chapter Eight
Learning to Let Go 85

Chapter Nine
The Must-Have School Supply 97

Suggested Reading and Other Resources 109

About the Authors 111

Chapter One: False Ideas We Believe

It's the first day of school and everyone is excited—new backpack, new shoes and new notebooks. It's a day of fresh beginnings, with a wide uncharted path ahead. However, depending on how those twelve years (or more) go, your child can either gain a strong foundation for success or graduate without all the necessary life skills. As teachers, we see a lot of mistakes that loving parents make, unwittingly causing a weaker foundation. This book is all about helping parents see the consequences of the decisions made in those early grades, and giving them a guidebook for connecting successfully with the school, the teacher and their child.

We all carry different experiences and memories that shape how we view what's happening in our child's classroom. Sometimes this happens for the better, and sometimes for the worse. Our false ideas—or even outdated ideas—can cause us to respond in a way which might be wrong. We need to be alert to how our childhood might be influencing how we are responding today. Ask yourself, is your mind blinded by the past? Some people are trapped by unhappy experiences, some blinded by happy ones. Pray for fresh insights into your child's educational experience. You might begin to recognize you have some false ideas. Here are some of the more common false ideas we have run into over the years that might have you trapped.

False Idea # 1

Johnny will learn everything he needs to know at school.

Wouldn't that be ideal? And indeed, some students can and do absorb the majority of their content without much work outside of the classroom. However, many students need extra time outside of school to practice and retain what they are learning.

A prime example of this is a student who knows his math facts. I remember: when I was younger, my mom drilled me at the dinner table on my math facts. This practice gave me an extra boost of confidence in a subject that I found difficult. Similarly, practicing sight words drills does the same for reading and fluency.

There are so many skills that children need to learn before they become adults. School covers many of the basics—math, history, reading, etc.—but learning should continue after the school day ends. A trip to the zoo with your child can become a learning experience if you talk about the animals' habitats or diets. A night at a play can bring up conversations about story structure.

If your child has an interest in art, music, acting, etc., then look for opportunities to broaden her horizons outside of school. The hours your child spends in a classroom does equip her with a lot of basics, but can't encompass every single thing she needs to know. In fact, a classroom could be seen as a place where students have come to learn how to learn.

False Idea #2

I don't have to be enthusiastic about the homework.

What attitude does your child see you project toward school work? Remember, the parent's attitude sets the tone for how their child perceives their work. Something that's become apparent to me over the years is that it is necessary to always remind our students, "to do all things without grumbling or complaining." (Philippians 2:14). However, hearing myself repeat that phrase, year after year, really brought my attention to my own struggles with complaints. Through prayer, I've had to work on my own negative habit of grumbling.

> The parent's attitude sets the tone for how their child perceives their work.

www.nowscpress.com/abc

One instance that comes to mind is the annual science fair. Everyone knows it's coming, and for some it's a real drain. The words you say about a project can influence how your child feels. Your approach can help or hinder how much your child buys into to the project. I remember one mom who looked forward to the science fair because she was excited to find a new and unusual question to answer. As a result, her daughter was also engaged, and it gave them good memories together.

As Galatians 6:7 says, "Do not deceive yourselves; no one makes a fool of God. A man will reap exactly what he plants."

False Idea # 3

Johnny goes to school only for the purpose of academic.

In reality, school is a microcosm of the real world they will one day face. They are practicing how to handle conflict, make friends, be patient, work together… and the list goes on. Every year, we take our students on a field trip to a place that's set up like a town. The students have to work and manage money. All the while, they have to work with other employees from both our school and others. It's interesting to observe students interacting as though they were adults. This scenario brings out how their personality would handle real world situations.

School is a great opportunity to learn. Not just for academic purposes, but how to get along with others, handle conflicts, how to be flexible without compromising integrity, and what to do when you don't get your way. There are so many valuable life lessons to learn within the school setting. As a parent, I see it as another aspect of how school shapes them.

False Idea # 4

Johnny's behavior will be different in school than at home. Or, the opposite—Johnny's behavior will be exactly the same in school as at home.

We once taught a student who was prone to disorganization. The parent complained about her daughter suffering the consequences of this struggle when she didn't turn in her schoolwork due to having lost it. However, when pushed, the parent did say this was a problem at home also. Characteristics true at home do carry over to school.

That being said, we have seen the reverse. One time at a parent conference, a mom was lamenting how her son gave her quite a bit of trouble over completing work. She was surprised to find out her son did not display that attitude at school, but worked diligently and happily.

The takeaway here is if a teacher mentions a struggle she has seen, whether or not you've also noticed it, don't be afraid to acknowledge it. As a united front, you can work together to help the situation, whatever it may be.

While your student may be spending 6-7 hours with his or her teacher, it doesn't mean she is the parent. At home, parents should be teaching manners and respect for authority. The teacher will come alongside you in this effort, but that is ultimately your responsibility.

Learning good manners will not only benefit them in the classroom, but also later in life. It puts other people at ease and makes them feel comfortable around you. One way to teach manners is to be a good role model to your child. Praise them as you see them display good manners and behavior. Use opportunities to instruct them on good behavior.

False Idea # 5

Johnny received a bad grade! The teacher must have dropped the ball. Johnny received an A. The teacher must be A-mazing.

Just because your child received an A in previous years, doesn't mean he will always receive an A. The grading rubric might be different, with the range of higher letter grades shrinking and opportunities for easy credit disappearing. The work may be getting harder for your child and now he needs to put in more effort. As fifth grade teachers, we see this last happen most frequently. The amount of unfamiliar contents increase with each grade.

One year, after our first spelling test, a parent approached me upset over her child's grade and remarked, "She's never gotten anything but a 100%!" The grade itself wasn't even an issue. The parent was used to a certain level of achievement—and expected it to continue. However, after the child recognized that she needed a little extra work, and consequently adjusted her study techniques, things were fine.

Elementary school is a great place to begin the pursuit of learning and growing, rather than just achieving the grade. There are many excellent opportunities to teach perseverance and determination, including those days when your child is faced with a bad grade or difficulties mastering the content. Perseverance and determination are habits that will benefit him in the long run, even if he does get frustrated sometimes. God's word tells us that perseverance is often what is needed when confronted with a new skill to learn (Romans 5:3-5). If your child wants to blame the teacher, reassure him that his teacher is there to help him and wants to see him succeed.

> Elementary school is a great place to begin the pursuit of learning and growing, rather than just achieving the grade.

During these hard situations, pray to the Lord with your child. This will train him to always remember that He is the number-one help in difficult situations, and can give your child the power to stay steadfast in learning a new task. When you see improvement, praise him for working hard and remind your child to thank God.

False Idea # 6

The teachers are out to get me.

Sometimes you will have to help your child overcome false ideas he has about his teachers. One common belief we've heard over the years is paranoia that teachers are specifically playing favorites and targeting other children.

I recently had this experience with my own son who, after having accumulated some discipline points, had convinced himself of this. For the most part, teachers are not going into the profession eagerly awaiting the day for their first demerit. With my son, I knew this was not the case, because the demerits were warranted, given the behaviors he was displaying. Through some questioning, I tried to help him see how he had believed this false idea. I knew he was convinced when he apologized to his teacher.

We do want to recognize there are some "bad apples" within the teaching profession. My own elementary school teacher, for instance, told my parents that the reason I couldn't read was because my parents didn't love me. This was certainly not the case, and she had clearly misjudged my family. You are your child's advocate and ally. If something is off with the teacher, it is your right to speak up.

It's important here to pray for discernment. After that, pay attention to any patterns you are seeing. If there is a consistent problem, go and see the teacher.

False Idea # 7

I can drop off my kids, head to the gym, and forget about everything until it is time to pick them up.

Your involvement is influential and impactful. It helps when a teacher knows you are involved and concerned with your child's education. At our school, we frequently have parents who are on campus; some ask how they can help their child succeed; some ask how they can help us; some simply try to connect with us. On the flip side, we sometimes run into families that we hear nothing from until the last week of the quarter, when grades are due, and then they only want to know how to bolster a grade.

Your involvement is influential and impactful.

Our chapter on Your Presence is Powerful will give you more insight on how to get involved. It shows your child that their education is important to you, and that's an attitude that will translate through your child and into the classroom.

What Matters Most of All: Note to Parents

A Be knowledgeable about what your child is learning at school. Ask questions about what he/she needs to study. Don't just take their word for it. If your school has an online homework program, make sure to utilize that so you know what assignments are coming up. If you have time, prepare in advance so you can be conversant when difficult subjects come up.

B It's good to start equipping your child with how to handle sticky situations within a classroom environment. Ask questions like, "What would you do if…" and share scenarios from your childhood. This is also a good opportunity to point out when your child needs to get help from an adult.

C Recognize your child's characteristics, both the good and the bad. Ask God for clarity on how to partner with the teacher to help overcome any characteristics you want to overcome.

D When your child receives a low grade, resist the temptation to assume the worst. Instead, get to the bottom of why your child received the grade he did. Was your child overconfident and simply did not study? Did he need help and did not ask for it? Were there careless errors made? Was the test harder than expected?

E One of the best things you can do is pray for your child's teachers and include your child in this practice. This will benefit the teacher, and help take away negative thoughts and perceptions.

F Look for ways to make your presence known. Introduce yourself to the teacher. Don't assume they know who you are.

G Kids need to be taught a number of skills, including making and maintaining eye contact, being a good listener, waiting their turn, and responding to adults.

H Help your kids build habits of prayer: pray with your kids before they leave you in the morning or on the way to school.

I Keep a family prayer journal. Kids like seeing results. Seeing answered prayers makes it more tangible.

Chapter Two: Your Presence is Powerful

So many of us set big goals with good intentions and high enthusiasm. For instance, maybe one day you decided you want to enter a 5k running race. You're not a runner, but you've got the motivation to cross that finish line. So you buy the brand-new shoes, the sweat-wicking shirt, you've downloaded a running app to humbly brag about how many miles you're running each day, and you've mapped out a training plan for the weeks leading up to the race. As teachers, we look at the school year in much the same way. You and your child are excited as summer edges toward fall and that first day approaches. You send your baby girl off on the bus, to a new grade, a new teacher, a new experience. You're both ready to seize the opportunities ahead. A few weeks later at the first open house, you sign up to be the homeroom coordinator/room parent, join the PTA, and start making friends with other families. Your child has a new backpack, shoes, and stain-free clothes. It all looks bright and shiny and hopeful.

With your running goal, the training that started out so fun and optimistic begins to change. Your shoes get dirty, the "likes" on your running posts dwindle, your muscles ache, your motivation dwindles, and the scenery of your mapped three-mile loop becomes familiar and boring. You begin to get tired, weary, and wonder if training will ever end, if it's ever going to get easier, and whether you'll be strong enough to finish the race. That's how you might feel about being involved as the school year progresses and as your child advances to higher grades and the demands on your time increase. In some ways, you will find your child's elementary years seem never-ending like those last miles; however, looking back you'll be surprised at how fast they went by. Just as there are times during a race when you want to simply stop, there are times during your child's education where you will want to drop out and disengage. When this happens, look to Isaiah: *"But they who wait for the Lord shall renew their strength; they shall mount up with wings like eagles; they shall run and not be weary; they shall walk and not faint."* (Isaiah 40:31)

> Being involved as a parent is critical to your child's educational victory.

Being involved as a parent is critical to your child's educational victory. We teachers cannot stress that enough.

Why Should You Get Involved?

Truthfully, if you're reading this book, we are confident you already value your involvement. Studies confirm how valuable parental involvement is. The Southwest Educational Development Laboratory found that students with involved parents, no matter their income or background, are more likely to:

- **A** Earn higher grades and test scores, and enroll in higher-level programs.
- **B** Be promoted, pass their classes and earn credits.
- **C** Attend school regularly.
- **D** Have better social skills, show improved behavior and adapt well to school.
- **E** Graduate and go on to post-secondary education" (Dervarics and O'Brian).

(Source: http://www.centerforpubliceducation.org/Main-Menu/Public-education/Parent-Involvement/Parent-Involvement.html) Your involvement communicates to your child that school is important.

From our personal experiences, we discovered that parents who are more involved in the school inevitably connect with others and become part of the school community. They interact and form friendships with other parents, which in turn often helps their child make connections with other kids. Children who have positive relationships with other students *want* to come to school because they can see and socialize with their friends. By building a support infrastructure with other parents, you have a resource for help at a school event, someone to go to when your child forgot an assignment's parameters, and another perspective on the classroom and the teacher. There will be some difficult moments along the way: a teacher unexpectedly quits mid-year, you discover your child has a learning disability, or your child is struggling with peer conflict. Your parent support network can help you navigate through those moments.

How Do You Get Involved?

Some time ago, I got involved in helping a church event; and afterwards they asked for our feedback. I had several opinions on ways they could change it, and I stepped up to be part of the core leadership the following year. In order to enact improvements, and better a part of your child's school, you have to jump in and volunteer, give and get involved. Be part of the solution. Schools rely on parent volunteers to support and build excellence.

Often the best schools have the most active and vibrant parent volunteers willing to step up and offer to do a host of tasks. They get the job done, whether it's fundraising, special ceremonies, or big events. Your volunteering conveys you are interested in helping to create an A-plus learning environment for your child and others. It may seem overwhelming to volunteer on top of raising a family, working full-time, chauffeuring to athletic practices, but it doesn't have to be. There's a place for everyone.

Ask the Lord and wait on Him to show you how you can contribute that year. There are plenty of ways to serve in your child's school. Just ask!

Some Ideas for Involvement:

If you're a leader:

Look for positions where you are coordinating events, be it Grandparents' Day or the Fall Festival. Step in to efficiently run this and delegate responsibilities. Or if you are just assisting the leader, speak up if you see things that need to be adjusted for the event to run smoother.

If you're artsy/crafty:

Go to the art teacher, and ask what events he/she may need help on. Volunteer to help decorate or lead the craft for classroom parties. This doesn't have to be anything elaborate or tough. We once had a parent hot glue forty pompoms to the end of our dry erase markers. Every year, one parent decorates the bulletin board outside my classroom. It was a huge help and she liked knowing she contributed in some way to our classroom. Ask the office if they need help doing the boards around the school hallways or decorating for school events.

If you're a reader:

First stop: library/media center. See if your school librarian/media specialist needs help keeping the books organized or needs you to help with a book drive. See if your school has a book club, or offer to come in and read with kids who need one-on-one assistance. Your child's teacher may need help getting their own library organized or someone to organize a drive to bring in new books for the classroom. Finally, in the lower grades, teachers often have guest readers come in to read to the class.

If you're organized:

See if the school office uses volunteers. An organized person makes a great homeroom coordinator. You don't have to do it all, you just mobilize the troops. That's where that network of other parents come in handy, to help pull off the bigger classroom events.

If you're hospitable/social butterfly:

Our school is really making an effort, along with volunteer parents, to set up events throughout the year to connect parents of students across all grades. Not all schools will, of course. Perhaps your school needs someone to step up to the plate? If it's feasible, approach the principal about ideas you have to organize events like a movie night or dessert social.

If you work/have limited availability:

Ask the teacher if there are things you can do from home. For example, one big time-saver for us is having a parent sort a curriculum we use every year. Organizing things like the Scholastic book orders seems so easy, but can be time consuming. Offering to do that is a big help to the teacher.

If you have marketing skills:

At set intervals throughout the year, most schools will do a fundraiser. Coordinate with local businesses for donations or sponsorships. Talk to a printing company about T-shirts for an event, or a big raffle prize. Use those marketing skills to get the word out to the media and to other parents in the area.

If you are a techie:

This is a valuable skill. Can you make the end-of-the-year video? Or run the media at the next special event? Or on a bigger scale, give a presentation on cyber safety to the students?

Keep your eyes and ears open for opportunities to contribute to your school. Whether you enjoy being large and in charge or behind the scenes, there's a place for you.

Be sure to recruit others to help. Not just because it's a lot to shoulder everything, but also because when your child graduates to the next grade, there will be a void left behind. In Ecclesiastes 4:9, God tells us, *"Two are better than one, because they have a good return for their labor: if either of them falls down, one can help the other up. But pity anyone who falls and has no one to help them up."* When I approach a parent about being the homeroom coordinator, I usually suggest another person they can ask to help them. I've found a parent is more likely to say "yes" when they know they won't be doing the job alone.

So far, we've focused on volunteering and connecting with other parents. There are other ways that your presence can be powerful. To make the most of these years, you have to be present for your child. When your child is young, he might need you to be a homework helper. Homework helper doesn't mean homework doer. It means you clarify, redirect, and encourage your child's thinking.

Homework helper doesn't mean homework doer.

There are several theories in the parent and education world about the value of homework. Too much? Not enough? None? However, if your school assigns homework, your child needs to complete it. If you feel like the amount is excessive, schedule a meeting with the teacher. One thing to remember is that homework should be a window to what is being learned in the classroom.

Math is one of the areas where we hear a lot of parental feedback. We don't teach math the way you learned it. New research in education has brought up better ways of communicating the complexities of math. If you are confused when you are helping your child, search the internet for a how-to video on YouTube or email the teacher for clarification. Don't be afraid to put a little note on the homework paper that your child is struggling with the concept.

Remember, homework doesn't just help a student practice a skill, it also teaches him responsibility and accountability. Even if your child says he did all his homework in class, we highly encourage you to do periodic checks just so you're familiar with what he is studying and how he is doing. It keeps you in the loop.

Being present means sometimes being your child's advocate. No one has more power to advocate for your child than you. When would your child need an advocate? Is it when she is encountering a bully? When he's struggling to keep up in school or complete homework; when he feels like his teacher is treating him unfairly; or when he is struggling with his peers and having social problems.

> Being present means sometimes being your child's advocate.

Your child needs to know that you will fight for her. Just knowing Mom and Dad have their back imbues children with confidence and support. There's a balance between growing independence and advocating. When should you intervene? When your child's learning is suffering, when she's in danger physically and/or emotionally, or when you see her shutting down. However, if your child is upset over a teacher's consequence, or a social offense that's a one-time incidence, first try talking about that at home.

An advocate is one who pleads the case of another. Present your child's needs and hear what the teacher has to offer. You might need to consult other resources like a tutor or educational therapist if you suspect a learning disability, but again, here, the teacher can be a great help in directing you.

However you choose to be there, ultimately being involved in your child's education sends him a message that your child is important, and his education is important. It will give you new and expanded ways to bond with your child and also keep you plugged in during those younger years that pass much too fast.

What Matters Most of All: Note to Parents

A Seek the Lord's direction in ways to be involved each school year. If you're burned out on being homeroom coordinator, don't be afraid to say no or try something different. Also, don't underestimate the importance of being involved.

B Remember your involvement matters. Whether you are at school or home, your child sees your participation and that's what matters. It sends him the message that it's important to connect with school.

C If you don't know what to do, ask the teacher. See what their needs are. Or go to the PTA president, the principal, or the specialist teachers (PE, art, library, etc.).

D Start or join a prayer group for your school.

Chapter Three: Developing a Positive Mindset

In my fifth-grade math class, we have some pretty tough skills to cover throughout the year. Each year, I introduce how to solve fraction word problems and model the steps on the board. Quite a few students became exasperated, saying things like "I'm never going to get this," or "I'm not good at fractions," or "Fractions just aren't my thing." These negative messages impact them in more ways than they can see in the moment. Developing and maintaining a positive mindset can make all the difference.

> Developing and maintaining a positive mindset can make all the difference.

My frustrated students are like people who come to a roadblock—the new function in mathematics, or, more generally, whatever is unfamiliar and new when introduced—and they either lose faith or give up trying to get to their destination. Others, though, decide to follow the detour signs and the unexpected twists and turns to eventually arrive at the place they want to be.

www.nowscpress.com/abc

Some students see setbacks or struggles as a challenge that can be overcome by effort and practice, while others do not. Helping students develop a positive mindset, so they can tackle those challenges successfully, is part of my job as a teacher and part of the parents' job. In the classroom, we try to remind students of other daunting subjects that they eventually mastered, and help them see that this tough problem is one they can conquer. It takes patience, and being willing to try and fail, before they can find success.

See how all these things interrelate? The ability to try and fail, and get up again, coupled with letting your child attempt new things on his own, feeds into helping him develop a positive mindset.

"I thought these were so hard at first, but they don't seem that way anymore," one of my students said one day. We discussed how, when faced with new and challenging tasks, we need to remember that our initial ability to understand the problems doesn't determine our success in solving them. How can this positive thinking impact your child's success?

Academic Success

The way you view learning and intelligence can determine how well you will succeed.

There is a critical focus right now in education on the term "growth mindset." Those who hold that a growth mindset is key argue that the way you view learning and intelligence can determine how well you will succeed. In simple terms, let's say you face a failure, like a bad grade, someone with a growth mindset would look at that bad grade as a setback, rather than just as a failure.

They would examine and analyze what they did wrong and use it to approach the next assignment differently in order to succeed. They'll try studying harder, meeting with the teacher, or studying with a tutor, whatever it takes because they have the mindset that with more effort, practice, and help they will eventually "get" the task at hand—or, that, at least, it will be a learning experience to grow from. They request feedback to trigger new ideas and help them see where they went wrong.

Someone with a fixed mindset looks at the bad grade as one with no room for growth. Essentially, that's how well they can do, and that's that. They don't, or can't, see other possibilities, because they see only what is present; and they don't like to face challenges head on for fear of failure. They might even be embarrassed by the grade and not want others to know about it. This is based on research by Stanford psychologist Dr. Carol Dweck over the span of 30 years. She coined the terms "fixed mindset" and "growth mindset" in her book, *Mindset: The New Psychology of Success*. Educators look at her research to see how to encourage the learning process versus just focusing on the end product.

One time, while I was teaching early American inventions, I assigned my students to present a skit about their inventor and product. They had very clear guidelines on what to include and what level of involvement was expected. Despite this, one of the groups found this task very challenging and were off to a slow start. They had chosen to do their skit on Robert Fulton's first American steamboat, "The Clermont."

Outside of school, however, they ended up banding together and allowing their creativity to overcome their doubts. On the day of the presentations, they arrived with a 5-foot model of the steamboat. One of the group members had decided to work on the project at home, and combined it with his passion for building. The model took their presentation to a whole new level and everyone's enthusiasm ramped up. Positivity is a mindset like this that we try to develop in our students by our classroom practices, but sometimes finding that is simply up to them. This student could have just thrown up his hands and said this isn't my type of project, but instead he found a way to make it work for him.

Including STEM (Science, Technology, Engineering and Math—a hands-on approach to learning that integrates all four areas) into the curriculum is important in education, because STEM is one of the primary means of evaluating schools. Students are often given a problem and must come up with or build a solution to the problem using a limited amount of resources and time. These types of activities can be very stressful to some students as they require a lot of higher-level thinking. The challenge can also be really exciting because it's outside the realm of what they usually do.

One day in the science lab, we were building a model of the ocean floor with the supplies we had available. One group of students complained that they did not have enough of one particular supply to be able to finish their model. As a result, they kept telling me, "We don't have enough. We can't finish." They dug in their heels, and at the end of the class, they had an incomplete model. On the flip side, another group had the same problem but worked around it. Instead of spending time to complain, they spent their energy coming up with a new idea. They were able to complete the model despite having the same problem as the first group.

These groups had different mindsets. The first group had a fixed mindset. They were frustrated, fighting, and gave up easily despite having feedback from the teacher. They couldn't seem to get past the initial setback. It's interesting to note, this was a group that was comprised of top-scoring students. In Dr. Dweck's research, she suggested that students who were seen as smart were sometimes hesitant to do anything that risked them losing their smart status. Perhaps, then, with this group, they didn't want to risk an alternative approach that could possibly fail, because they thought failing with the standard instructions and insufficient material might not be seen as failure.

Developing a growth mindset takes time and it's important for teachers and parents to model this for the child. How do you do this? Focus on the process of learning, rather than grades or results. One way to do this is to praise her for her effort, as opposed to talking about how smart she is. Effort is something she can control. Being perceived as making an effort comes as a result of making an effort; being perceived as smart comes as a result of chance or nature. Effort-based compliments include the following:

Focus on the process of learning, rather than grades or results.

"I can see you worked so hard."

"Way to keep trying!"

"You sure challenged yourself."

Another step toward a growth mindset is to acknowledge the importance of mistakes. Your child won't always come home with an A, and this is not necessarily a bad thing. There's a lot that can be learned through an imperfect grade. Instead of just looking at grades, try to look at what your child is learning from the assignments. When he is discouraged, tell your child about times you have failed and what you've learned from those times. That will show your child that mistakes are a necessary part of learning.

If your child is old enough to understand, talk to her about the fact that when you are learning challenging new material, your neurons are building new connections because dendrites are reaching out to other dendrites, which causes your brain to grow stronger—like how using muscles builds and strengthens them. The great thing is we live in a time where there are YouTube videos showing this concept in kid-friendly language. It's an empowering concept for your child to learn, unlike when we were kids and our IQ tests determined how far we could go, limiting some children by labeling them as low IQ, and declaring others failure for having a high IQ and not being successful.

Another important step is to help your child learn to reframe her thoughts and statements. Frequently we hear our students say, "I can't do that!" "It's too hard!" or "I'm not good at math." When you hear your child say things like that, don't reinforce that language by saying things like "I'm not good at math either." Instead, open it up by saying something like, "I had to train my brain at math." Or "I'm working on getting better at math." Acknowledge that math was—and, perhaps still is— a struggle, but you persevered. Another great tool we use right now is teaching our students to add the word "yet" to the end of these defeating sentences, "I can't do that, yet." It reminds them they are in the process of learning a new concept.

A good way to promote mindset is through literature. You should read books with your child and when you see examples, growth mindset or fixed mindset, talk about the advantages and disadvantages of each. As a reading teacher, my students will often point out examples they find of these mindsets in the main characters without prompting. Some examples of books you can look for at your local library are *The Girl Who Never Made Mistakes* by Mark Pett and Gary Rubinstein, *The Fantastic Elastic Brain: Stretch It, Shape It* by JoAnn Deak (Ph. D), *The Dot* by Peter H. Reynolds, and *The Most Magnificent Thing* by Ashley Spires.

Outcomes are weighty, because, in the end, grades do matter too. All through the school year, we should look for that energy expended on learning to produce an improved understanding; the improved understanding will—or at least should—in turn, cause a better grade, product, or level. Keeping a growth mindset is never easy, because we have to develop the habit of continually evaluating how our practices encourage the child to grow, test boundaries, explore, fail, grow and learn. We do the best we can in the classroom and we encourage you to bring the practices into the home, because they encourage the mindset which best encourages a child to grow and learn.

Work Ethic

By modeling a strong work ethic at home, and nurturing it in your child, he is much more likely to develop a character-defining habit that will serve him well at home, in school, and in his adult life.

One simple work ethic practice you can do at home: in lieu of simply providing privileges and possessions, have your child earn them. It will help your child see that hard work is valuable and through that, she will experience the feeling of accomplishment. It will also allow her to learn delayed gratification, which is an important concept in today's instant-everything world.

Nowadays, children are used to instant gratification. If they want to see a movie all they have to do is hop on the TV and stream it. Teaching delayed gratification and earning what they want promotes a strong work ethic. Students need to see the value in the process of learning and working. Without a strong work ethic, we see kids these days wanting an easy "A" in class. As teachers, we try to combat that, but it needs to start at home.

> Teaching delayed gratification and earning what they want promotes a strong work ethic.

Some time ago, while teaching second grade, I had the students do a dinosaur project. The students each researched a particular dinosaur, created a board or diorama, and presented the information to the class. The children were given a checklist of all that needed to be included in their final project. As you imagine, there were a range of grades received based on this rubric applied to the quality of work turned in. One student's project lacked several components and the overall quality was poor; therefore, he did not receive an A. When returning the grades, the student was clearly upset and questioned what happened. We went over the criteria; and, together, we noted the elements he was missing. The disappointed boy admitted his project was started and finished the weekend before. He rushed to get it done and didn't have time to finish all the requirements. It was a good teachable moment on what good a work ethic looks like.

How do you recognize a strong work ethic when you see it? Children with a strong work ethic have a sense of responsibility. They want to succeed in school; they take ownership of their work. They want to complete things to the best of their ability, whatever that may look like. Second, they demonstrate self-control. They have school and work as a priority over talking to their friends during class. They can resist the temptation to be lazy with a big project and they have learned to spread out the workload over several days or weeks. Third, these children are diligent. They work to the best of their ability, turning in thoughtfully completed work.

We aren't looking for every student to be exactly the same; rather, we are looking for them to do their best and to put in the time and effort needed to create quality work. With the above student, his work wasn't his best nor was it high quality, something he acknowledged. Had he taken more time, he certainly would have been one of the top-scoring students.

Finally, and most importantly, we are looking for honesty. We want students to do their own work, get help when they need it, and be willing to take risks with independency. All of these elements come together to form a positive mindset, which creates a positive learning experience. It fosters more interest in education and thus, more success—a win-win all around!

What Matters Most of All: Note to Parents

A Use positive language. Remember the power of *yet*.

B Encourage the process of learning versus always emphasizing the finished product.

C Share examples of your own mistakes and what you learned from them.

D Have your child earn their privileges.

Chapter Four:
Maintaining the Joy in Perseverance

Every year our school enters a big writing competition. I lead the students through the process of writing a narrative story. We write, edit, peer review, but inevitably there's always one where the student has this amazing story that abruptly ends with, "I woke up and it was all a dream." Maybe he got tired of writing and just called it a day. A short story is comprised of a lot of words, and writing that many pages can be daunting. Persevering through to the end and giving the last pages as much strength as you gave the first pages can be tough. However, reaching a strong and satisfying "the end" can have a huge impact on your child today, and far down the road.

How do we teach our students the joy that comes from persevering to the end? How do we show them it's important to not only start strong, but finish strong? Some of us might be thinking, *how will I do that, when I struggle with that issue myself?* Should we really be surprised when our kids want to take the easy way out when we see in our own lives all the times we've done just that?

I remember reading a blog post about a mom who decided one May to raise the white flag of surrender. In her funny, tongue-in-cheek way, she proclaimed she was done in the month of May—done with the lunch making, the schedule keeping, and the crazy running around.

Trust me, teachers feel that way in May, too. By that month, the end of the school year is close, but not close enough, and sometimes we're all in survival mode. As difficult as it is, you have to shift your thinking to be more present, instead of focusing on getting to that last school day. That helps you and your child maintain his joy, and heading into summer knowing the vacation was well earned because she finished strong.

> As difficult as it is, you have to shift your thinking to be more present, instead of focusing on getting to that last school day.

What is joy? Joy and happiness are often used interchangeably, but there is a fundamental difference. According to Aristotle, "Happiness is the meaning and the purpose of life, the whole aim and end of human existence." Pleasure and delight are fleeting emotions, though they simulate happiness closely enough that we commonly call them happiness. I feel delight after my students do well on a test, after we eat cookie cake together, or when I'm hanging out with my cats. Joy, though, is the supernatural pleasure we have in the presence of God, being completely who we are in Christ. It is knowing that despite our circumstances, we have eternal salvation in Christ.

There is joy found when you persevere to the end because perseverance is the ability to continue trying to do something even though it is difficult. I remember a friend taking on a huge responsibility that was going to require a lot of hard work and difficulties along the way. I asked her if she was excited about the new position. She said that she wasn't particularly excited about all the hard work, time, and mental energy it was going to take, but she did have a joy knowing she was doing what God had called her to do and she was looking forward to the new challenge.

It's rare to find a student who is eager to put down the iPad, the basketball, and the American Girl doll to get to their homework. It's going to take a change in attitude and a focus on the big picture—on that feeling of accomplishment and joy he will find when he finishes his assignments. James 1:4 says, "Let perseverance finish its work so that you may be mature and complete not lacking in anything." We know your child will face challenges, but developing a perseverance mindset will help.

Triumphant Finale

"Don't count down to the end of the year, build up to a finale," says Noah Geisel. I don't want any of my students, myself, or parents waving a white flag of surrender until the last bell has rang, and then I want it to be a flag of victory. It's easy to lose sight of what matters most of all in the daily grind or just as school year is wrapping up.

Throughout the year it might be hard to keep the joy, hopefulness or excitement of the new year. Your child is tired and he begins to grumble, he doesn't like school, he doesn't want to go, he doesn't like his teacher. In the Bible, God gives us many examples of His promise to help us go through the holes in the fences of life. God promises that our trials can purify our faith and refine our character. Your child may find himself discouraged and defeated when she gets several bad grades, when there has been miscommunication with the teacher, or when she falls behind due to illness or something else.

The great apostle Paul did not let any obstacles and adversity, whether being flogged, shipwrecked, imprisoned, or beaten discourage him from his course to spread the gospel in Rome. Leaning on Peter's words: *"Be truly glad there is wonderful joy ahead even though you have to endure many trials for a little while. These trials will show that your faith is genuine. It is being tested as fire tests and purifies gold- though your faith is far more precious than mere gold. So when your faith remains strong through many trials, it will bring you much praise and glory and honor on the day when Jesus Christ is revealed to the whole world."* (1 Peter 1:6-7)

When your child is going through a hard time at school, it's important to take these situations to the Lord in prayer. Model to your child how to pray through these situations. Remember that God will use challenges to build character **through** perseverance.

One year, we had a student who was struggling academically. By the fourth quarter, his grades had slipped considerably and his parents wanted to take action. They were confident that with some extra studying and hard work, he could pull his grades up before the end of the quarter. They decided he should study during recess in lieu of playing, with a stiff ultimatum of what would happen if he didn't and his grades didn't improve. For many fifth graders this would be the end of the world as they know it, but this child really took it well because he was also committed to finishing strong. He wanted to turn things around, and knew this was the only way to do it.

When students dismissed for recess, he would come up and ask, "What can I study for class today?" At one point, he even said, "I know I can do this," despite how dire his grades were looking at the time. Even though he did get teary-eyed at times because of how hard it was, he stuck with it and didn't give up. In the end, he accomplished the goal. Like the verse, he was tested and purified through this experience. I have no doubt that God used this season in his life to build

> *Remember that God will use challenges to build character through perseverance*

his character and teach him a lesson that he will lean on in other similar situations.

If your child is struggling, teach your child how to make a plan. If her grades are suffering, decide on some steps she needs to take in order to improve. It was easier with the student above who was determined to fix the problem. Truthfully, that's not always the case. We often see students who can identify a problem, but they don't know how to fix it; or don't want to, because the steps are hard. Don't wave the white flag just because your child complains. Your child will need to be encouraged and cheered on how to persevere just like we all do at times. Encouragement might even come in the form of identifying some rewards along the way for improvement.

God promises that obedience brings joy: *"Oh, the joys of those who do not follow the advice of the wicked, or stand around with sinners, or join in with mockers. But they delight in the law of the Lord, meditating on it day and night. They are like trees planted along the riverbank, bearing fruit each season. Their leaves never wither, and they prosper in all they do."* (Psalm 1: 1-3)

Your child will be faced with assignments she doesn't want to do, rules she doesn't want to comply with and procedures she doesn't understand. Try to help her see that rules are there for a reason, and that disobedience or "bucking the system" leads to bad consequences. God does promise when we obey all will go well with you (Deuteronomy 16: 18). Sometimes we don't have an external reward for good actions, but we still have the peace and joy of knowing we did the right thing in the eyes of the Lord. We can know that we have a clear conscience when we are being obedient. In our classroom, we teach the students a little jingle about obedience because we feel so strongly on the topic. It goes something like this, "O is for Obey, O is for Obey, Obey is doing what God says, O is for Obey."

If your child is repeatedly breaking the rules or disobeying the teacher, examine what is at the heart of the disobedience. His actions could be rooted in a lack of self-control, disrespect for authority, pride, troubles at home that are impacting him emotionally, or trouble in school that he hasn't shared. Work with the teacher and ask if there's a particular time or place where your child is routinely disobeying. Are other children involved? How is your child reacting? From this and frank conversations with your child, you may begin to detect a pattern that will help you in the plan.

> If your child is repeatedly breaking the rules or disobeying the teacher, examine what is at the heart of the disobedience.

Attitudes are contagious, and maintaining a positive one can make a big difference. There are several disappointments that can occur throughout the year and become attitude deflators. Like a big balloon that slowly loses air becoming smaller and smaller, each disappoint can begin to deflate our attitude. It's hard to keep up a good attitude. No one is always at a top level of excitement all the time, but we also don't want to go so far down that we throw in the towel. You can take to heart these words: *"Be strong and courageous, and do the work. Don't be afraid or discouraged, for the Lord God, my God, is with you. He will not fail you or forsake you. He will see to it that all the work… of the Lord is finished correctly."* (1 Chronicles 28: 20)

Your attitude impacts everything you do. As we write this, I'm reminded of a parent whose child had real academic difficulties. However, she was the most upbeat, uplifting mom. She stayed involved in schoolwork and didn't give up on finding the best resources for her son. She also really made an effort to encourage the teachers. Thus, she was really a bright spot for us to be around that year. We saw the same attitude in her son. He was a real joy to teach despite his academic struggles.

It's also good to know who your child is spending time with at school and the influence that child is having on your child. Help your child make the connection of how her friend's attitude is affecting her. You might need to practice with her about how to handle when her friend has a bad attitude or says something negative. One trick is trying to return your friend to a "happy" place by asking a question like, "Remember when we did that fun science experiment?" Remembering good fun times can turn around a sour attitude. Another is dropping someone from the status of friend to acquaintance—or stranger—when it becomes clear that the friendship is not useful, does not bring happiness, or improve goodness. Removing toxic influences from your child's circle can turn around a negative attitude.

As hectic as your mornings are, try to send your child to school in a good mood. Maybe you've had one of those mornings where everyone woke up late, someone couldn't find a shoe, or the laundry with the uniform pants is still wet in the washer, and the whole family is frazzled and rushed. It's hard to have joy on a morning like that, but take a moment before school to pray. On the drive to school, turn up the radio to that upbeat song to turn the mood around. Wave good-bye with a smile, a hug, and an "I love you!"

> Removing toxic influences from your child's circle can turn around a negative attitude.

Perhaps you only have to look in the mirror to discover the source of your child's bad attitude. It's okay; we can all look back to a time when we reacted in a way that contributed to our child flying off the handle. Your attitude can be the thermostat in your child's response to a situation at school. When your child brings home a special project to complete, or a book to read for that book report, what vibe are you sending off? Are you annoyed or frustrated? Remember, kids are intuitive. You may not like the work, but they don't need to pick up on that because your attitude could become theirs. Then it becomes exponentially harder to get the job done. Now you aren't just fighting the project, but you are fighting the bad attitude about the work.

"Show me the right path, oh Lord; point out the road for me to follow… the Lord is good and does what is right; He shows the proper path to those who go astray. He leads the humble in doing right, teaching them His ways." (Psalm 25: 4, 8-9) We once talked to a mom who realized her choices were negatively impacting herself and her family. We began to see her overreacting to minor situations and not handling them well. She seemed stressed and burnt out; and it was impacting her child not just at home, but in school too. She confessed that she needed to make changes and choices for her child's sake, leaving more time for school and being a kid. These are tough conversations to have, but they are necessary. For this family, it wasn't an overnight change, but the gradual shift did help alleviate some of the stress and her child responded by being more joyous in school.

When you feel like giving up, remember that God gives us strength in the midst of our weariness. The calendar is jam packed. It seems like every day after school there is something to rush to or stay up late for. The hopes of having family dinners turn into pulling into the nearest drive through fast food restaurant. Homework, sports practice, art classes, and family engagements are overwhelming. Hold on to this verse when it seems like the dam is about to break loose, *"…I will strengthen you and help you. I will hold you up with my victorious right hand."* (Isaiah

41:10). We have limitations, but God does not. And when we follow the path God has given us, sticking to it no matter how hard the road becomes, there is always joy to be found at the end.

What Matters Most of All: Note to Parents

[A] Fix your eyes on what is eternal. The day-to-day grind will always be there. If you stay focused on God's promises, you can see ways to glorify Him in even the most mundane routines.

[B] Identify the heart of your child's disobedience and attitude. This will help you determine your next steps. Make a plan.

[C] Evaluate your choices throughout the year to see if they are beneficial. What things are you tightly holding on to that you can let go of? Maybe you need to try something new. Ask a friend if you are stuck in a rut about how they would handle your situation and see what you can learn.

[D] Joy is the gift we receive when we rely and trust His promises.

Chapter Five: Helping Your Child Develop Good Peer-to-Peer Relationships

There are days in my classroom when I'm faced with such a barrage of "he said/she said" cases that getting to the bottom of the conflict could have qualified me as a full investigative detective, or even an FBI agent—some of the disputes seem that big to the children involved. Sometimes my head is left spinning at the end of recess after the countless number of conflicts I have had to solve. Peer interactions define a child's school day, and can provide a help or a hindrance to your child's academics. They are also a great learning and development moment.

It doesn't take long into the school year before your child comes home and says: a fight happened with a friend at school; he and his friend aren't talking, and he doesn't know why; he is stuck in the middle of a disagreement between two friends and doesn't know what to do. He doesn't want to betray any of his friends and it's all just confusing. With a potpourri of personalities in a classroom, it's not surprising that eventually students have conflict with one another. So, how can a parent uncover just what is going on? If only, like on those crime shows, you could run the data through the magic computer and get the solution.

> With a potpourri of personalities in a classroom, it's not surprising that eventually students have conflict with one another.

Too often, we see parents who are either afraid to step in and come into the school, or outraged and sure that their child did no wrong, or, sometimes, unwilling to accept that their child could be a victim or the perpetrator. They refuse to see that there are two sides to every story and, sometimes their child was the instigator, and sometimes not. It can be hard to accept that your son or daughter is picking on another child, or was the first one to get into a scuffle at recess. It can also be hard to accept that your child is consistently a victim. We understand. We try to gently guide parents around the event—or, frequently, pattern of events—to understand what really happened. We see it happen often: a parent is adamant their child would never throw a punch, but after talking to their child they wind up returning, having to admit that indeed their child not only fought, but started the fight. So talk to the teacher, talk to your child, and try to look at all sides of the story.

Open Mindedness

What we wish we could tell parents is this: be open-minded when it comes to other peer's relationships with your child. No child is perfect; and, in most situations, there is blame to be had on both sides. Try to step back and look at the situation with an impartial eye, and counsel your child from that viewpoint. Part of growing up is learning where you are lacking, what areas most need work.

Helping children get along with others and have positive peer exchanges takes wisdom and guidance. Our children live in a #SELFIE world where they are bombarded with the messages that they are number one. The message—with a thousand faces—is on t-shirt slogans, advertisements, and in television shows they see every day. Without proper guidance from parents and teachers, our students' peer relationships will be adversely affected by this message. To oppose this message, children should learn early on to think less of themselves and more of others. As God's word tells us: *Do nothing out of selfish ambition or vain conceit, but in humility consider others better than yourselves.* (Philippians 2:3)

Humility is a recognition of one's defects, and an acceptance of one's relationship to God and to others. Putting humility into practice means being honest with ourselves, looking inside to find our own fault in the matter at hand, and then offering understanding to the other person. You, as the parent, have to help your child learn how to do this.

Start by teaching your children that conflict is an opportunity to display Christ-like characteristics. Give them opportunities at home to practice putting others first: being the last one in the car, doing a nice deed for a sibling or neighbor, or letting his friend choose his flavor of popsicle first. More to the point; make it a rule at your house that during play dates, the friend chooses the first activity. Reinforce this behavior with praise, or a small reward. More importantly, when your child chooses to put others first on his own, praise your child for making that choice. The practices your child learns at home will develop into habits which carry into school and with his peers.

Traditional Bullying

The buses have barely left the parking lot when we get a phone call from an irate parent who is upset over a situation her child had with another student. She is rallying the teacher to get involved and threatening to call the principal. She's already texted another parent to gather intel from another child.

This is where we need to say, 'pump the brakes and take a deep breath.'

We've all had moments we've overreacted. In those moments, it can seem best to turn to oneself—and perhaps others, if needed—to solve the problem. But, before taking any action, take it to God first. Asking for wisdom and discernment from God is essential. Let your child know you are praying about what she should do about the situation. Ask God to show you through a message or verse on how your child should handle the conflict at school and whether you need to become involved.

I know a parent whose daughter was facing a somewhat unusual circumstance at school. The girl's peers would offer her a potato chip and just as she would say "yes" the peers would lick it and start to giggle. As the taunting went on for a couple of days, she had to tell her mom about it. This wise woman told her daughter that they would begin by praying about it and see what God would have them do. The daughter wanted to avoid her mom going in to address the problem and be perceived as a snitch. The next day, while pondering the situation the mom's mind moved to Proverbs: *If your enemy is hungry, give him food to eat; if he is thirsty, give him water to drink. In doing this, you will heap burning coals on his head, and the Lord will reward you.* (Proverbs 25:21-22)

With this thought, the mom asked God to show how her daughter could show kindness to the girls taunting her daughter. God gave them an idea, one based on Christ's teaching of passive resistance, where by not responding in anger, one reveals to one's oppressor their cruelty and appeals to their humanity or sense of shame to change: *You have heard that it was said,*

'Eye for eye, and tooth for tooth. But I tell you, do not resist an evil person. If anyone slaps you on the right cheek, turn to them the other cheek also. And if anyone wants to sue you and take your shirt, hand over your coat as well. (Matthew 5: 38-42)

The next day, they packed some extra cupcakes in her lunch for the girls. When she offered them to the girls, they were excited. At this moment, my friend's daughter asked, "Would you like them licked or not licked?" Of course, they replied, "not licked" and, as they said this, the sudden insight spread across their faces as they recognized what they had been doing was wrong. My friend's daughter replied, "Good, because that would be germy, and I know my dad wouldn't like that."

The girls clearly received the message. They shared a special treat together and the problem was resolved without the mom having to intervene at school. Often, we want to react quickly to a problem, like by telling the daughter to just sit somewhere else at lunch or calling the parents of the other children in anger. If we model to our children how to take it to the Lord, be patient in our response, and to trust His plan we teach our children a valuable lesson on resolving conflict. In this story, we see Luke modeled: *Love your enemies, do good to those who hate you, bless those who curse you, pray for those who mistreat you.* (Luke 6:27-28)

One-Time vs. Ongoing Offenses

There will be times when you have to evaluate whether the conflict your child describes is ongoing or a one-time offense. When it's an offense that is uncharacteristic of the other child, then it's good to advise your child to brush it off. Ask your child, "Could it be possible your friend behaved the way she did towards you because she was having a bad day? Could you forgive her and ask the teacher to be merciful in any punishment?" Satan would love for us to live perpetually offended and for the cycle of injury and revenge to remain unbroken, but these are moments when your child can learn to start practicing compassion for others.

On the other hand, there will be times when the conflict is ongoing. This is when you should mention it to your child's teacher. You can alert the teacher to something for which he needs to watch; likewise, the teacher might have some observations he can share with you.

Bullying is such a difficult topic, and one we deal with in the classroom. Children can be cruel to one another, and the long-term effects of bullying can be devastating. If your child is the one being bullied, talk to him often, get the teacher involved, and try to work out some conflict resolutions. And, whether your child is bullied, or simply sees it happening, teach your child to speak up, because keeping the bullying silent often encourages it to happen more.

Your Child, the Bully

What if your child is the bully?

Parents never want to think that their child is the one hurting others in the classroom. You must, however, be realistic and listen to the teacher's viewpoint with an open mind and heart. If your child is hurting others, it's important to get to the root of why as early as possible. Very often, when children lash out at others it is because they are trying to cover over their own hurts or selfishness. It takes honest, frequent communication and, sometimes, the intervention of a professional therapist, to get to the root of the problem and set your child on a healthier path.

Don't be a parent who buries her head in the sand. Some parents pass it off as "normal" or allow their child to play the victim role. They'll say, "Boys will be boys." Teachers deal with parents who blame everyone and everything—from the way the teacher starts the day to where their child's desk is located to the color of the paper on which handouts are printed, for their child's behavior. It's easy to want to shift blame to someone or something else for your child's behavior. But your child is responsible for his response. He might have only contributed a small portion to the conflict, but he needs to own that portion and deal with the consequences.

Your Child, the Peacemaker

If we could have one overall message, it would be this: Be honest.

Be honest with yourself.

Be honest with your child.

Be honest with your child's teacher, too.

Heading off these issues when your children are young helps them grow into strong, compassionate and courageous adults. Teach your child now how to be the peacemaker in a conflict. This doesn't mean being a doormat, letting others treat him unkindly or unfairly, rather, it means learning to display a Christ-like character during conflict, forgiving persecutors in order to break the cycle of hatred, and in so doing, honor God.

Model being a peacemaker at home and share stories of times when you deliberately chose to be the peacemaker. Admit that the path of the peacemaker is not the easy one, and that it is hard to allow your friend to have his way when they remain blind to what you are trying to make them see. Share stories from the Bible of people who chose to be peacemakers; Abraham giving up his rightful position as elder to allow Lot to choose the best land; David sparing a vengeful Saul when he had the chance to kill him; and Ruth taking Naomi's nation, family, home and God for her own, and rejecting the nation, family, home and gods with which she grew up. Christ suffering death for our sins. In the same way, our children can give up their right to have the first cupcake and curb the urge to say an unkind work in retaliation to an unkind word said to them. And whether they win or lose at kickball, chess, or swimming; or whatever their sport or game of choice: teach them both the courtesies of victory and defeat, that is, magnanimity and graciousness. God provides the power for your child to live by putting his peers first. Christ-like character is built one decision at a time. The more we help our children practice this, the more it will become a natural response during a conflict.

Peer Pressure and the Art of Thinking Biblically

As your children age, peer pressure takes on much darker tones. Most of us want to fit in and feel accepted by others, which can lead to making poor decisions. If you do not teach your children techniques to handle the need to feel accepted when they are young, the consequences when they hit their teen years will be unpredictable and devastating. Parents need to help children learn the necessary social skills to navigate the complexities of the world: how to resist negative peer pressure; how to stand firm in their values instead of compromising to fit in with others; how to accommodate others without compromising their integrity. Our children might desire to please man before God, but we know God delights over a choice or decision is the only one that matters.

Memorizing God's word will provide your child the moral reserves to stand firm against negative peer pressure. God will call those verses to your child's mind when he has a problem or is tempted. By knowing God's word, your child will know God's standards and what He expects from him. You cannot expect your child to *act* biblically if she does not know how to *think* biblically.

> You cannot expect your child to *act* biblically if she does not know how to *think* biblically.

My mother-in-law had a little girl in her class who was being teased by one of the boys. In reply, the girl exclaimed confidently to the boy, "I will have you know I am fearfully and wonderfully made!" Just like Jesus, she responded to her mocker with God's word. Is that not better than retaliating with an abusive word or throwing a punch? This child had an identity in the Lord, which was so deeply rooted in her soul, that she was able speak it with confidence to her persecutor.

There will be days when your child is mocked for his beliefs. There will be days when your child feels lost and abandoned by God. There will be days when your child wavers in his belief and strength. You have to be there then, to shore him up, and to remind him of how fearfully and wonderfully made he is, and that he will get through this, and to the other side.

In addition, you can help him have a positive self-identity in himself by encouraging and developing his unique gifts and talents. Whether it is sports or writing or horseback riding or sewing, support your child in these areas. Give him that feeling of uniqueness. Your child will grow stronger by excelling at what he loves, and that will be another piece of armor in the war against peer pressure.

Those are the things that will strengthen your child when a group of friends or classmates encourage him to get into trouble. Pulling a prank or cutting school or hurting another child—whatever the goal of the group, it can be hard to stay firm in convictions in that moment.

This is when you need to talk to your child about consequences and how his choices affect others. Encourage your child to stay away from those kids because those friends will not lead him in Godly, Christ-like ways. God does give the strength to resist temptation. One of those ways is to simply ask God to remove you—or remove yourself—from the occasions in which temptation is near. Selecting peers to hang around who make good choices is important in helping your child to stay focused on learning. It can be tough for kids to see the big picture, but as they make one decision after another that impacts their life in a positive manner, they will gain that necessary vision.

Sometimes when our children stand firm in demonstrating Christ-like behavior in peer relationships, it will separate them from others who are not making the same choices. Your child may have a season where he feels isolated and lonely, cut off from the little community he has built up over the school years. This is when you support him, help him choose activities and friends who bring him closer to God, not further away. As hard as it is to see your child hurting, it is *failure* that builds our strength, not success. At the same time, continue to be gracious, kind, and loving to the students who have excluded or been mean to your child. Seeing your kindness, your child will learn how to love his enemies by imitation; hearing you pray for those students even though they have not treated him well, your child will learn to pray for those who persecuted the by imitation, teach him compassion and grace in your words and deeds.

> Help him choose activities and friends who bring him closer to God, not further away.

Social Media

In an age of social media and immediate cell phone access, this can be a massive challenge. The phone in your child's book bag allows you to contact him; it reassures you he's okay; it also carries many dangers. Children are exposed to social media at an earlier age, often before they are ready for it. Conflicts begin small: a cruel word in a text, an exclusion from a group message, or a photo of a birthday party from which only one or two were excluded. Then they grow and fester on social media, eventually erupting in the classroom.

It's hard to monitor all that our children are doing on their devices, but there are apps, parental controls, and checks that can help us. Restrict your child's screen time and set boundaries—decide if it is even necessary that he have a smart phone, or if a flip phone will suffice. Trust your intuition as well. You need to know the passwords. If you sense your child might be involved in a bad situation, then you are more than likely right. Do some digging. If you uncover a concerning text or picture, don't be afraid to confront your child. Determine whether you need to mention something to the other parents, and what exactly that is. Even though it might be uncomfortable to inform another parent about their child's involvement, wouldn't you want to know if it was your child?

I had a gut instinct not too long ago that something was happening with my child on social media. Sure enough, a parent called to tell me of an incident her daughter had told her, involving my child being catfished by some other students. I reached out to the parent of the instigator. Thankfully, in this case, the parent was open to hearing the truth of the matter.

This isn't always the case. There are parents who turn a blind eye and can't imagine their child being the ringleader, or even tangentially involved. You have to look at this through a lens of honesty—children are curious, children can be cruel, and children are tempted to break the rules. Continued honest dialogue is key as well as boundaries. When this happened with my daughter, I took her off social media for a time; because, even though she wasn't the instigator I could identify poor decisions she had made that opened her up to this. Cyber bullying, sexting, and exposure to strangers are happening more frequently and at younger ages. So, parents, you need to be alert and vigilant. Form their habits in virtue well: every decision you make, every lesson you model, is necessary for them to flourish as adults.

> You have to look at this through a lens of honesty—children are curious, children can be cruel, and children are tempted to break the rules.

What Matters Most of All: Note to Parents

A Don't be judgmental (lest ye be judged). Be open minded with new peer relationships.

B Don't be afraid to communicate if you believe bullying is happening.

C Look honestly at your children in bullying situations, sometimes behavior might be hidden.

D Try to model being a peacemaker at home.

Chapter Six:
No Kid is Perfect

In the beginning of the school year, our favorite read-aloud is *Be a Perfect Person in Just Three Days* by Stephen Manes. It's a great opener to school for a myriad of reasons. The basic plot: a child, Milo, finds a book that will help him become perfect; however, it teaches him that it is both impossible and boring to be perfect, because in order to be perfect, you would have to do nothing. If you are doing anything—from washing a dish to folding your clothes—you will be imperfect. Milo discovers individuality is not just more interesting than perfection, but also more fun and realistic. It's the same in the classroom. There's this image of the perfect student—one who is always on time, completes all assignments and gets an A on every test.

The truth is, kids are as human and fallible as the rest of us. There is no perfect student, because we all have strengths and faults. Helping children learn to capitalize on

> The truth is, kids are as human and fallible as the rest of us.

their strengths and work around their weaknesses shows them that they don't have to be perfect to be successful.

Tips for Success

Attendance is important, including being there for the full day. September is Attendance Awareness Month, which encourages schools and communities to remember that engagement matters for attendance. It's not just about being in that seat every day, it's about learning to be responsible and that school is a priority in life.

According to Attendance Works, a national and state initiative that promotes better policy, practice, and research around school attendance:

- **A** As many as 7.5 million students are chronically absent nationwide. That includes one in ten kindergartners.

- **B** As early as pre-K, chronic absence predicts poor attendance and academic performance in later grades.

- **C** Poor children are more likely to be chronically absent and more likely to lose ground academically.

- **D** By 6th grade, chronic absence is a leading indicator that a student will drop out of high school.

E By 9th grade it becomes a better predictor of dropout rates than 8th grade test scores.

F Classroom turnover from too many absences affects all students, even those who attend regularly.*

Although it can be tempting to take your child out of school for a day at Disney or an early family vacation, it's important to make going to school a priority. What message do you send your children when you allow them to miss school frequently for fun activities? Set the expectation that showing up at school every day will make a difference. Also, before the school year begins be clear on what defines a sick day. This helps you not to give in to minor complaints.

One time I was teaching with a bad headache, and I left right as the kids were dismissing. One of the students realized why I left so fast, and the next day said, "I can't believe you taught all day with a headache!"

I replied with, "Well, that's life. Sometimes you just have to work through the pain." Just as sometimes you have to go to school when you are tired, when you've had a bad day, when you have the sniffles or when you feel unprepared. These are lessons kids have to experience because they will carry over to their adult life.

---

* http://www.attendanceworks.org/wordpress/wp-content/uploads/2016/02/Brochure-8.5x11-revised-2016.pdf

We do know there are unavoidable absences due to sickness and special life events. When this occurs, there are steps you should take. Be sure to contact the teacher and the office to let them know what's going on and how long you think your child will be out. Make arrangements to get missed work. It's not always possible for them to make up hands-on activities and projects, but ask if there is something comparable he can do at home. Stick to a schedule to get the missed work done, and once your child goes back to school, have them double-check that everything was made up. It can seem overwhelming to your child to have several days of classwork to finish, but help them take it one chunk at a time.

The second component, which goes hand in hand with attendance, is preparation. It doesn't do much good to sit at a desk without books, paper or writing instruments. We have students who really struggle with being prepared for class, losing things, and being organized.

If you see your child is disorganized—forgetting materials, losing assignments, or forgetting to turn in assignments—don't just simply attribute this to laziness and wait for her to grow out of it. If it's affecting their academics, she needs help from you and/or the teacher. One approach is to make a plan with the teacher to help empower your child with strategies to organize herself. Ask for your child's input in creating an organizational strategy that works for her. This helps her to take responsibility for her own organization, because it is hers: she owns it and thus tends to then put in the effort.

Set up routines in your home to manage the school paperwork: write events on the calendar; note deadlines; clamp permission slips and notes together on the refrigerator. Organize the various papers in folders so your child's binder can focus on class work instead of being inundated with everything else and so he doesn't miss important due dates. Some schools have procedures where they send everything home on a particular day; but, if your school doesn't, we recommend you select a day—once a quarter, at least—to make sure to empty out any papers you see. When they're younger, you may be checking their folder more often; but, as they progress through school, you should back off as they step up in responsibility for their assignments. Also, if your school has an online portal for homework, make sure to check it, so you can catch any assignments that your child may have missed writing in his schedule. Keep a visual calendar of due dates at home so your kids remember what is coming up.

As teachers, we really enjoy students who are teachable. What do we mean by teachable? Teachable students love learning; they are curious; they are receptive to feedback. The love of learning is something that cannot be taught, only fostered. From the time your kids are little, when

> Teachable students love learning; they are curious; they are receptive to feedback.

they show interest in a topic, do what you can to help foster their curiosity. For instance: we had a student who had some learning disabilities, but her parents had really fostered a curiosity by giving her new and unusual experiences. She had gone to space camp, our local science museum, and her family had planted a butterfly garden. All of these experiences provided her with knowledge that she could connect to learning at school. She would regularly contribute interesting facts that she had picked up along the way.

While not everyone can do big things, the internet can provide virtual experiences. I know one child who engages his science interest through listening to podcasts his mom has downloaded through an app called Stitcher. There are many technological tools we can use to spur deeper thinking; but, on the other hand, too much technology can interfere with a teachable and curious spirit. We strongly recommend that you set limits on your child's screen time. They need to also experience the living world in order to grow interest in it. Ask God to give you opportunities to prompt their interests and inquisitiveness. I know a mom whose daughter loved horses, but they could not afford for her to take lessons. She and the daughter prayed for God to open a way for her to be able to take lessons. They decided to go to the local horseback riding place and ask if she could clean the stalls in exchange for horseback riding lessons. The owner agreed and she spent many afternoons after school with horses. Today, she is in college pursuing a veterinary degree.

Parents also dream of having a perfect child when their baby is born. We imagine him as a star football player, a lawyer, a doctor, or a business executive. While it's good to have expectations and dreams for your child, always also be open to new dreams and possibilities. When he starts school, you might be tempted to start playing the comparison game when you talk to other parents. The comparison game can be tricky, because it either leaves us puffed up, feeling like our child is ahead of everyone, or failing as a parent, because it seems like our child isn't measuring up. Our pride can be passed on to our child through our contemptuous attitudes and words, or we can project our humiliation through our envious attitudes and words. In either situation, we harm our child by trying to make him be something God did not intend. When we do that, we rob ourselves of seeing the qualities that God has given our child. There is no perfect student or child; rather, each has his own special gifts and talents from God. Trust that God has equipped your child with the characteristics and interests needed to fulfill His plan.

> There is no perfect student or child; rather, each has his own special gifts and talents from God.

What Matters Most of All: Note to Parents

A Try to schedule appointments and special events when children are not in school to limit absences.

B Set up a morning routine to help your child (and you) be on time for school. Cushion your travel time to expect delays.

C When your child is absent, help him to stay on top of his work. Take it in small chunks if there are several days' worth to catch up on.

D Implement clear procedures and routines that keep your child organized. Involve him in the process so he knows what's expected and feels a sense of responsibility.

E Be purposeful and intentional in creating moments that will engage your child's brain. See what your child is interested in and what you can do to cultivate that. Think outside the box.

Chapter Seven:
Communication is a Two-Way Effort

Picture it; we've all been there…

Your kid goes to school one day and is "surprised" to see everyone else dressed up for the day in costume. Or picture day arrives and you find out after your son comes home in a stained T-shirt. Or maybe there's a field trip, and your child misses it because the permission slip never made it home.

We are fortunate to live in a climate where communication is readily accessible. Between texting, email, social media, you can make contact with the press of a button. But for all of that, there always seems to be miscommunication. People get busy, they forget, things get misplaced. Your child is coming home with a pile of papers, and one permission slip or flyer can be easily missed. To avoid this pitfall, try to stay plugged in and remember engagement matters for your child's success in school. Communicating with the teacher is one way to partner with the school to make the most of this academic season. Remember it goes by fast.

Guidelines in Communication

As the start of school nears, you receive communication giving you the dates for "Meet the Teacher" and "Open House." Both of these are important events to attend as they are packed with essential information to get your year off to a well-informed start. First impressions are vital, and they set the tone that you are involved in your child's education. Teachers appreciate the families who attend even if it's your third, fourth, or fifth year with that teacher. The teacher will communicate important events, milestones, curriculum notes, as well as what to expect for the coming months. It is a great time to meet the teacher so he or she can begin to connect your child's name with your family. If you cannot attend, the next best thing is to contact the teacher: introduce yourself, express your disappointment in the fact that you are unable to come, and see if there's a time that works for you to just stop in and meet the teacher.

Next, attend parent-teacher conferences. As fifth grade teachers, we often see a trickling off of parental attendance. We would encourage you to make sure to keep attending these throughout your child's education. Your child's teacher is preparing for your conference whether you show up or not. They have tips for you, knowledge about how your child is progressing, and strategies to improve his academics and in-class behavior. Remember, you see your child as themselves, but teachers see your child in comparison with the rest of the grade. They know the benchmarks your child should be meeting.

If the school has days scheduled for these conferences that do not work for you, contact the teacher to set up another time. Another option is to do a phone conference. Or if you feel like you need a conference sooner than the dates suggested by the school, reach out to the teacher. Your involvement is what matters to the teacher, not how it happens. If you can, prepare questions ahead of time. We recommend the following as a starting point, but feel free to come up with your own specific to your child:

> Your involvement is what matters to the teacher, not how it happens.

What should I do at home to help support his/her learning?

The teacher may recommend extra resources or books you can use at home to help. These aren't required but will prove beneficial to support their learning.

How is my child doing comparatively?

As mentioned above, the teacher sees your child in relation to many others. As a consequence, she will know whether he is hitting benchmarks at an appropriate rate.

What are my child's strengths/weaknesses?

You know your child best. However, the teacher may be seeing some reasons behind why he is performing the way he is. For instance, maybe his Social Studies grade has taken a dip because he is struggling in reading comprehension, or having trouble seeing, or falling asleep during that part of the day because he isn't getting enough sleep at night. Asking about strengths and weaknesses can help reveal underlying areas or issues, and also give you a starting point for helping your child.

How is my child doing socially?

The teacher can tell you how your child handles himself in group settings, whether he generally acts as a leader or follower. If your child plays alone, does he do that by choice or because he was excluded? What is his characteristic means of handling conflict in the classroom? Your child's ability to do so should mature as he does.

Does he/she stay on task?

Your child should be able to start and finish classwork on time. The teacher will be able to tell you whether he is getting distracted, the work is too hard, or he is not putting in the effort. You may already know he is struggling to complete work, but this is a good opportunity to find out what the teacher thinks the reason is.

May I share a concern?

This is a great opportunity to share any concerns your child may be experiencing. If something negative has been happening, the teacher may simply be unaware; this meeting is a good opportunity to share what is going on. Teachers want to resolve problems before they escalate. Avoid being confrontational or defensive when sharing these concerns. Make a plan to resolve the issue, follow it, and meet again to discuss the results.

I'd like to fill you in on something…

We know this isn't a question, but during conferences, this is also a good time to let the teacher know of anything significant that might be impacting the child emotionally. Is your family going through a divorce? Have you recently lost a loved one? Have you been victims of a crime? These are hard topics to share, but they will impact how your child is feeling and thus how he responds in the classroom. So it is a good idea to let the teacher know.

When You Have an Issue with the Teacher

You pick up your child; he slumps in the car and begins to cry.

"What's wrong, baby?"

"I lost recess because the whole class was misbehaving at lunch."

This has become a pattern in recent weeks. Immediately, red flags go up in your mind and you begin questioning. "What were you doing at lunch?"

"I didn't do anything."

After a long car ride home, you are both upset and frazzled because it sounds like your child was singled out. You decided that you ought to write an email to the teacher. But wait, don't shoot off that email in anger! You're not sure you agree with how the teacher handled the situation, but you begin to realize a cooling off period and time to reflect is in order.

First, ask God to give you wisdom about how to best handle this. After you've cooled off and prayed, contact the teacher first. There is a chain of command to follow and going straight to the principal or adding the principal to the first email jumps over the teacher. The principal may need to become involved if the issue is not addressed, but the first contact is not the time to involve him or her. When contacting the teacher, you should do the following:

Ask for clarity about the situation.

Ask, "Can you tell me what happened?" When you do this, instead of starting off with, "I don't like the way you handled this," it sets a calmer tone. Sometimes, your child might be forgetting some of the important details, or simply be wildly inaccurate.

This forgotten information may help fill in the gaps for you. As Proverbs reminds us: *A soft answer turns away wrath.*

State your intention for the email, don't leave the teacher guessing.

Sometimes we get emails that come off very negative when really that weren't the case at all. It leaves us feeling defensive when the parent was simply looking for clarity. Don't say, "Why was the entire class punished today? My child was upset when I picked him up!" Say instead, something like, "My child is upset about the whole-class punishment that has been happening recently, especially the one that happened this last Tuesday. I'm wondering what's been happening."

Call to action

Ask what you can do to help your child. Do you need to meet with the teacher? Tell the teacher, "If the problem persists, please let me know."

Where to go from here?

You've sent your email, you got a reply, but it's not what you're hoping for. Where do you go from here? It's important to recognize that you have options.

You could set up a conference with the teacher. At this conference, try to go in with an open mind. Communicate what concerns you and what you want for your child. See if you can find middle ground, but be open to understanding the reasons behind the teacher's policies as well. Hold a mindset which looks forward, not backward. While it is unlikely that your meeting will change your situation, it might help change how things are handled in the future. Also, be ready to hear hard truths. You might hear things your child hasn't said he did—or hasn't done; or you might hear about the situation from a new perspective that broadens your understanding

We like to think that children are always upfront and honest; but, in reality, their recollection is marred through their experiential perspective, understanding, emotions, opinions, and imagination. Things won't change unless you speak up. A teacher will sometimes remain oblivious to a problem unless it is brought to their attention. An example: we get feedback on the amount of homework we give and we adjust accordingly.

I sometimes hear parents say that the reason they don't want to speak up is that they fear that the teacher will take it out on their child. Every time that fear is brought up at my school, we teachers have been quick to reject that notion. We welcome feedback. While, yes, this occasionally happens, it is not the norm with the majority of teachers who are dedicated to their vocation. If you feel your child is being unfairly targeted, then you absolutely need to take this to the principal—or higher, if the principal takes no action.

We strongly encourage you to focus on tone. Keep in mind, the more aggressive one party is, the more defensive another side becomes. The ideal situation is for parents and teachers to be working in concert with each other, making sure there is enough communication to be sure the child does not slip through the cracks.

If problems continue, then take a moment to hold off on starting a big email chain or group confrontation with the teacher. Instead, turn to your network of parent friends to discuss, evaluate and see the bigger picture. Remember your friends from volunteering for the school? They are the starting point of your network. Ask if they have had a problem similar to yours, and how responsive the teacher has been. Sometimes, sharing information can clarify matters.

After looking through the school's policies to see if any are being violated, perhaps two or three, working in good fellowship might go together and ask about the matter, if appropriate. If not, simply let the teacher know the impact of his decisions in the classroom on your children. If you don't get a response, take your group concerns up the chain of command.

On the other hand, you might even be tempted to go to last year's teacher or another teacher in the building to see if they agree with you. Do not do so. When parents criticize one teacher to another teacher, it puts us in an awkward position. It's possible we feel the same way you do, but want to remain loyal to our colleague and at the end of the day, we have to work together. We also aren't in the other classroom, and don't know all the details or variables. It's best just to keep us out of it. It's similar to a child playing one parent against another.

We sometimes hear comments like, "While at the birthday party, people were talking and…" There is an important difference between going to your close, valued friend for advice, and going to the masses to try to get people to see your side. If the issue has become one that has activated the parent network, now is the appropriate time to approach the principal with your concerns, assuming you have already talked to the teacher. The principal will be able to help you from there based on the school's policies.

Communication between Your Child and the Teacher

Often kids who have been out sick come in and ask about what they missed, before checking the online portal or the blackboard, or the note we sent home. Some students who miss a day or two of school are very diligent about getting their work; but, then, the reverse is also true. If your child can get on her phone to set up a play date with a friend, find the time to go to a ballgame/movie, and schedule a FaceTime with friends, she can find out what homework she missed. Especially as children advance in grades, the excuse of not being able to find out the homework wears thinner and thinner, because they have so many resources for information.

Communication at home also helps you to find out what's going on in school. Sometimes it takes more than the question, "What did you learn in school today?" Most students will say "nothing" or "recess was fun," and that's the end of the conversation.

Don't let the subject go so easily. Ask specific questions about his day in order to build your relationship with your child. Go through the schedule, class by class. Ask if the teacher said anything interesting or confusing. Ask what the assignments were. Ask with whom they ate lunch, and what they talked about. Ask what was confusing in their classes, and with whom they partnered with, etc.

> Ask specific questions about their day in order to build your relationship with your child.

Communication has multiple layers—between you and the teacher, the teacher and your child, your child and you. It takes effort from all involved, and questions that go further than the surface, to truly learn about your child and her school experience. Whether you're making casual conversation on the car ride home or after dinner, these give-and-takes are snapshots to the overall picture of your child's school journey.

What Matters Most of All: Note to Parents

A Go to the open house and parent teacher conferences. Introduce yourself to the teacher. Get to know the classroom, the expectations and the curriculum.

B Remember that your tone matters. Don't write something in an email that you wouldn't say to someone's face.

C Try to look at all sides before reacting.

D Follow the chain of command. If a concern arises, first go to the teacher.

E Help your child stay in the loop if he is absent.

F Keep up with handouts and emails from the school.

G Sign up with your school's social media or if they have text alerts.

Chapter Eight: Learning to Let Go

As parents, one of our biggest goals is helping our children transition them into adulthood. Despite that, it seems as though we see many examples of young adults who don't make this transition. These are the students who in their early years were not given the opportunity to learn responsibility and accountability. They are the ones whose parents rushed back to school every time their child forgot homework, lunch, or their band instrument. Your decisions now impact your child's later ability to "launch" and grow into a confident and independent adult. You can empower or enable your child. The choice is yours.

Setting Up Steps

As your child ages, look for ways to give your child responsibility. We have had students in the fifth grade who can't tie their own shoes, which is a task typically mastered by age 6-7. We are always left scratching our heads as to how a child can get to fifth grade without knowing how to tie their shoes, but perhaps all along it was "easier" for a parent to tie the shoe rather than to wait for their child to try. This basic skill is a pathway to helping a child learn that sometimes you fail many times before you succeed. Are you quick to jump in when your child has difficulty with a new task or skill? Give your child time to practice and master it on their own. Do you let your child go outside, fall down, get dirty, maybe a little scuffed up, then encourage them to get back up and try again? Falling down and getting up again is part of life and learning that now will go a long way into adulthood.

> Falling down and getting up again is part of life and learning that now will go a long way into adulthood.

In math class when we start a brand-new unit like fractions some students are paralyzed with the unknown. They often want all the steps done for them or lack the confidence to complete a problem independently because they are used to someone else helping them. On the other hand, students who have had the opportunity to fail and try again are more able to take on new tasks. As a result, they become more confident taking risks in the classroom.

First, start with small steps. Each time you give your child a new task to do, make sure you explain it to them clearly and also discuss why it is important. With laundry, for instance, show them how to sort their clothes, measure out the detergent and start the washer. After a few practice times, back off and let your child try. It's only laundry—failing isn't a big deal. Letting him learn from natural consequences is more powerful than stepping in to avoid or fix the problem. Resist the temptation to micromanage, whether it's with making a sandwich or building a tower out of bricks. In school, teachers let students try, and if the answer comes out wrong, we wait to see if the student can figure out the mistake on his own and correct it. If not, then we step in, but always trying to guide the child into figuring out the error, rather than telling them what went wrong.

Every child is uniquely made by God. However, there are certain benchmarks to look to obtain as they age. We urge you to use this as a guideline.

Kindergarten

At the end of the day, you are ready to pick up your little kindergartener. You know he's had a long day and you're excited to see him. Maybe he wants to just run off and play, leaving you to deal with his coat and backpack and the papers the teacher sent home. It can be tempting to think your little tyke had a rough day at school and it's easier to pick up after him, but don't do it. Teach them to take care of their things before they go play. It's about teaching your child independence and how to do things himself. It's another building block for launch. What seems like an easy or basic task to us is a big milestone in the life of a five-year-old child. Step back and take an inventory of things you are doing for your child that he can be doing for himself. Then launch!

1st Grade

As a first grader, their steps move more to schoolwork. They will need to be able to sit for longer periods of time. Every school is different; but, most likely, you will see homework that they will need to complete and be responsible for turning in. This is a key moment in setting up for future success. Don't procrastinate on homework; set up a routine to get it done before dinner. Setting this pattern early and sticking to it will hold your child in good stead down the road.

2nd Grade

Second grade is a wonderful year to see the lessons of kindergarten and first grade solidify. The students are feeling more confident and are used to the routine of school. In reading, make sure to have your child read to you or take turns reading aloud. This will help them practice reading with fluency and reading accurately with expression. Their reading ability will vary at this age so don't fall into the trap of comparing where they are with their friends. Help them to be successful, and if you aren't sure, remember to ask the teacher. Math facts are an important skill to master, so pick up some flashcards and practice throughout the week. You can even make it fun—at the grocery store, have your child add the number of cans or subtract the amount of a coupon. Making math fun and laying the groundwork of basic facts will be foundational as they move to higher and harder math. Today's headache to help your child learn these saves you a migraine in the future when the math problem involves multiple steps.

3rd Grade

Third grade is a big year. Students transition from "learn to read" to "read to learn", so your child should be able to read well on their own by now. If not, work with them more often at home, hire a tutor or have another relative work with your child on reading.

If you notice your good reader is bringing home bad grades, this might be an indication that while she can read fluently, she's struggling with understanding what she's reading. This is definitely a red flag that needs to be addressed with the teacher. Struggling with reading comprehension carries over into all subjects, particularly math and word problems.

A next step of independence is writing their homework assignments down and not being so reliant on an online homework portal. Children need to take responsibility for turning their homework assignment in to the teacher. If they miss turning in an assignment, they need to experience the consequence whatever that may be (low grade, missed recess etc.). It's better to learn these lessons now—in elementary school—than in high school or college. These are the life consequences that later ignite a successful launch.

4th and 5th Grade

For our fourth and fifth grade students, there is an increase in complexity of books, lessons and expectations. Big projects and papers are being assigned, with long-term goals and many short-term steps in between. This type of work introduces your child to time management. How do you avoid the all-nighter in fourth grade to finish the science fair project? By helping your child make a plan, and sticking to it. That means when your child receives an unexpected invitation to the movies, talk to him about what is on his plate that day and how those two hours at the movies will affect their To Do list.

The reality is that sometimes important things will be left to the last minute, but don't bail your child out by doing the project. Even if he has to stay up late, he can do it and still wake up with the alarm clock. By letting your child sleep in and go to school late, you're sending a mixed message about his responsibilities. As they grow up, deadlines are often not optional. You miss it, you are out of luck.

6th Grade

If fifth grade wasn't the last year in your elementary school, then sixth grade is. Sixth graders definitely want more independence, so it's important to help them navigate how to make all that work. Instead of waking them up, let them start using an alarm clock. If they miss the bus, allow them to suffer the consequences of arriving at school late. This is also a pivotal year for handing big assignments without parental involvement. Teachers assign projects that kids can complete on their own, so try to step back and let that happen.

Failure Is an Option!

So you've modeled how to study correctly, and your child does it perfectly every time, right? Don't we wish? When your child comes home having experienced failure, sometimes it's tempting to want to step in and "solve it." Maybe they forgot to bring their homework to school, so you email the teacher asking for grace. Perhaps they failed a test, so you come up with ways to get them extra credit. However, the hard lesson—for you as well as your child—is to let your child experience failure. **Failure is how we learn. When their parent** constantly steps in for them, the child becomes enabled. They become confident someone else will do the work for them and everything will work out in the end. When they are adults, this has devastating consequences. We know how hard it is to see your child upset, but truly, letting them fail will teach them far more than constant success. This is a big part of learning to let go, and stepping back to let your child fly on their own wings.

> The hard lesson—for you as well as your child—is to let your child experience failure.

Many schools have an automatic email system that sends grades daily. You see a bad grade, and might be tempted to yell at your child for not being ready for that test or accusing him of not studying enough. Take a deep breath…and respond, don't react. When a bad grade comes through, or a disappointing experience happens, instead of jumping in to solve it, talk through the situation with your child. Ask probing questions to see what they think happened and make a plan for next time. If necessary, talk to the teacher to make a list of concrete steps for the future.

The key is to put the power in your child's hands more and more as they age. In the early years, forgetting an assignment or not studying enough can be due to not being completely plugged in to how school works. But when your child is older, they know the routine and what is expected of them. Step back, let them go, and avoid the temptation to problem-solve everything.

Consequences

Something that we teach our students every year is that with every action there comes at least one consequence. Sometimes we will like those consequences and other times we will not. Letting go means allowing your child to experience consequences and learn from those lessons.

That goes for both good and bad events. Acknowledge when your child accomplishes a task well. Praise your son for being dependable. Celebrate good grades and hard work on projects. Also, remember to keep these goals towards independence enjoyable. Learning new skills is difficult for anyone, so if it is becoming stressful make sure to step back, pray and ask God for wisdom.

If your child is overall being responsible about getting up on time, doing his assignments and turning them in, forgetting to hand in an assignment once shouldn't be a big deal. Repeatedly forgetting to turn in homework should result in consequences, both in the classroom and at home. At school, your child might have to miss recess or receive a zero for the assignments. At home, have the conversation about why the homework hasn't been turned in, but have consequences if this is an on-going habit, like losing screen time or missing a favorite activity. You can also contact the teacher and work out a plan together to help your child get back on track. In the end, however, you have to step back as your child gets older, and allow him to have more control over his decisions. If he continues to make the wrong one, he will learn that the consequences are rarely worth skipping an assignment or not doing his best.

Sometimes handing out a consequence to a student is hard for the teacher. It's hard for me because I know it's hard for them, and like you, I don't like to see my students upset. A verse that encourages me during these times is, "No discipline seems pleasant at the time, but painful. Later on, however, it produces a harvest of righteousness and peace for those who have been trained by it." (Hebrews 12: 11) It's hard to give out consequences, but picturing the "harvest of righteousness" or the independent child of God they will become is the inspiration to stay focused on.

Learning to let go is a tough lesson, for you and your child. They're going to want to hold mom and dad's hand as much as you're not going to want to let go. But in the end, letting them have that independence will teach them so many valuable lessons and help them become stronger, more resilient and confident adults.

What Matters Most of All: Note to Parents

[A] Set goals each year for your child on what steps you would like them to accomplish. Ask them what they think.

[B] Throughout the year, remind them of those goals. If they are struggling with turning in homework on time, for instance, remind them how hard they worked on the assignment and how turning it in can set them up for success all year.

[C] Remember when they fail that it is not a reflection on you. Instead, take it as a learning opportunity for them. Sit down with your child and go over what happened. Make a plan for next time. If you feel like you need to, or if it is an ongoing problem, communicate with the teacher about how to correct the situation. Resist the urge to make the failure go away.

[D] Set clear consequences. Be clear about what will happen with ongoing negative behaviors.

[E] Praise good behaviors. Praise is just as vital and gives your child a positive tape to draw from when they feel discouraged.

www.nowscpress.com/abc

Chapter Nine:
The Must-Have School Supply

Every fall, schools issue a list of must-have school supplies; from pencils to notebooks, backpacks to tissues. Parents scramble to fill a cart with everything their child is going to need on the first day of school.

What do you think was the most important school supply you purchased for your child? Was it the cell phone to call you in case of emergency? Or the brand new super binder that has lots of folders and pockets to help him keep organized?

What do you think your child would say is the most important thing? Is it the cool pencil pouch, the popular shoes or the designer backpack?

The answer is none of the above. While the pencils and binders and cell phone help in the day-to-day activities, the best school supply you can give your child is one he can't buy. It's free! Now that's refreshing! I mean, look at how much you spent to fill his backpack with needed supplies. And half of them seem to come home at the end of the year unused.

School Is About More Than ABCs

The best go-to school supply is prayer. It's the glue stick that keeps you bonded to God, the ruler that measures your dependency on Him, the pencil that keeps you communicating with your Heavenly Father, and the lunch box that holds what nourishes and strengthens you for daily work. It's the school supply your child will not want to forget in times of trouble. The one supply that is always available to him, day or night, rain or shine. In large part, your child's understanding of prayer will come mostly from what he sees and hears from you.

Why do we Pray?

It's important that your child is learning to pray and looking to God throughout his day. He will have many opportunities to depend on Him for his needs and help. Talking to God recognizes His authority in our life. He is everywhere with us; an ever-present help in our lives. When we see answers to prayer, it's an encouragement to continue depending on Him through prayer. Prayer brings peace and hope to a troubled heart. Throughout their day, our children can walk and talk with the Lord and seek that peace. If they struggle with faith, help them keep track of the prayers that have been answered, and the surprises that have come at just the right time.

Commanded to Pray

Philippians 4:6-7 says, *do not be anxious about anything, but in everything by prayer and supplication with thanksgiving let your requests be made known to God. And the peace of God, which surpasses all understanding, will guard your hearts and your minds in Christ Jesus.* We are commanded in the Bible to pray, and to keep that line of communication with God open every single day.

Privilege

When my Grandmother was no longer physically able to help with the kids as she used to, she was deeply saddened. While she could no longer lend a hand with carpool or play with the kids, I knew she could still pray for them. I gave her a list of specific requests to pray for, for each child. Even from afar and homebound she still had a mighty way to participate in her grandchildren's lives and that gave her a deeper connection with them and with God. We are privileged to have a God who wants a relationship with us, if only we speak to Him.

Prayer Changes the School Experience

Prayer provides an opportunity to align our hearts with God's will and to be ready to stand on God's choice. Sometimes we are not looking at a situation correctly, but as we begin to pray, God will lovingly reveal a wrong motive, attitude, or thought and replace it with the right one. Have you turned to God in prayer in order to align your heart? It's like the child

> Have you turned to God in prayer in order to align your heart?

who has an enemy at school, and finds their heart beginning to soften because they have prayed for the other child. It's only through specific prayer that we see our heart being aligned to that of our Lord and Savior, Jesus Christ.

How to Teach Your Child to Pray

One of the lasting legacies we can give our children is teaching them to pray. Having a daily prayer practice at home will give your child the foundation she needs, and the confidence to turn to God when times are tough. Prayer is an all-encompassing anywhere, anytime supply.

Set the example of talking to God throughout the day. Be verbal in thanking Him, even for simple things like getting a green light or a good parking spot. When a need arises during the day, let your child hear you ask God for help, direction, and strength. Be sure to also model praise. Remember to praise Him for who He is and the gifts He's given you. This helps establish a thankful heart and an attitude of gratitude. Let your child know that you thank God for giving him to you and that you see your child as a blessing.

> When a need arises during the day, let your child hear you ask God for help, direction, and strength.

In turn, teach your child to be humble and grateful. One mom we know taught her child to say three things he was thankful for and three things he was sorry for at the end of the day. This took prayer beyond just "give me" prayer, where you are treating God like Santa Claus.

Teaching at a Christian school affords us the opportunity to pray with our students and their parents. On Wednesday mornings, we invite our students and their parents to join us in prayer with the fifth grade class. Jesus gave his disciples an example of how to pray in Matthew 6:9-13 when he prays what is commonly known as the Lord's Prayer. Before our first "corporate" prayer, we would teach the students the ACTS prayer as an example of one way to pray. We find it gives them a little more boldness to speak up. We start with adoration, words that say who God is. When we taught adoration, we wrote the alphabet on the board, and then brainstormed words beginning with each letter that described who God is. For example, A for all-knowing, B for big, C for compassionate, you get the idea. We teach the ACTS prayer—Adoration (Psalm 48:1), Confession (1 John 1:9), Thanksgiving (1 Thess. 5:8), Supplication (Phil 4:6-7)—in hopes of creating a lifetime of our students accessing the most powerful tool in their backpack.

With supplication, we saw our students had gotten into a habit of just asking for good health, grades, and safety for the troops. While it's good to pray for all those things, it's not always clear how those prayers are being answered because they are too general. It's easy to imitate another person's actions without really having a heart for what you are now praying.

Children need guidance in how to be more specific in their requests. We ask them to think about that day's schedule and any problems or challenges that arose over the day. Over the course of the year, the students grew in making the prayer time their own. Children became confident in praying in front of others and using their own words. They recognized things they could pray for that they hadn't before. Through these class prayer times, we were able to praise God for answers to prayer that had been voiced during these times. As teachers, we pray this leads to a lifetime of turning to God throughout the day with tasks and being comfortable with talking to Him.

We realize that being in a private Christian school allows us to pray for our students. But even when my children attended public school, I met with a group of moms once a week to pray. Our children knew we were praying for them and their school. Sometimes they would ask us to pray for a test they were worried about or a big assignment that was due soon. I also had another prayer group that couldn't meet because of conflicts in our schedules, so we exchanged index cards with prayer requests for our children. Knowing I had friends praying for my children gave me comfort and peace.

Prayer Schedule

Keeping a set time and a list of prayers will help both you and your child to pray consistently. Corrie ten Boom said, "Don't pray when you feel like it. Have an appointment with the Lord and keep it. A man is powerful on his knees."

We suggest one of the last things you do with your children before they head off to school is pray with them. We know mornings are busy, so these may be short and sweet. There are many patterns you can enlist to think through all the needs and concerns of your child. This isn't a strict list, but it may help you stay accountable and feel assured you are covering their day in prayer:

> We suggest one of the last things you do with your children before they head off to school is pray with them.

Pray that Your Child:

[A] Comes to love Jesus and God's word.

[B] Stays safe while at school.

[C] Shows kindness, compassion, and love towards others.

[D] Listens and respects authority.

[E] Engages in the learning and participates in classroom discussion.

[F] Admits he/she needs help and asks for assistance.

[G] Has and holds fast to a teachable spirit.

[H] Maintains effective organization.

- **I** Grasps new concepts and has a curiosity for learning.

- **J** Has eyes to see those who need help, and a willingness to serve the teacher.

- **K** Is patient with those who are different from him or her.

- **L** Flees from unsafe and bad situations.

- **M** Chooses friends who are a good influence.

- **N** Perseveres when the work is challenging, stays focused, and gives his best effort.

- **O** Responds to conflict in a Godly way.

- **P** Looks for opportunities to serve.

- **Q** Holds strong when others pressure her/him into doing wrong.

Prayers can become more specific as your child tells you about issues, due dates, and school events that are on the horizon. I know moms who start a prayer journal and record when and how the prayer was answered. It's a great reminder of how God was present and a source of help throughout your child's school year. Prayer gives our children spiritual strength to stand strong and prepares our hearts to hear God.

Not only is prayer the best school supply for your child, but the same is true for your child's teacher.

Pray that Your Child's Teacher:

[A] Loves God and His Word, developing a personal relationship with Jesus.

[B] Is given a loving heart for each child.

[C] Develops meaningful connections with each child.

[D] Shows wisdom in planning and instruction.

[E] Displays creativity in lesson planning.

[F] Has classroom technology that runs smoothly.

[G] Makes efficient use of time.

[H] Has strong behavior management, and deep insights into why a child might be misbehaving.

[I] Is given discernment on how to handle conflict between students.

[J] Is granted patience when students are struggling, and eyes to see methods to help.

Most parents have received the emergency call from our children that begin with the words, "I forgot…" Isn't it good that no matter what our children forgot to bring to school that through intentional training we can equip them with the greatest school supply that is always with them? Earnest and persistent prayer fully prepares our children for all that God has for them to do, encounter, and accomplish throughout their school day. So, as you toss the pens, pencils, paper, and binders into the cart this year, will you purposively make sure you give them the most important one?

We believe in building relationships—with our classes, with the parents of our students, with God—and helping our students do the same. In the end, it comes down to compassion and communication. Coupled with prayer and a strong reliance on God, your child's school years can be some of the best years of his life. And that means those fresh beginnings, with the new backpack, the new shoes, and the anticipation, will carry through all twelve years of school and long into adulthood. School will be more than just an education—it will be an experience that shapes your child into a strong, confident and capable adult.

What Matters Most of All: Note to Parents

A Be a prayer paramedic. Pray daily yourself. It will be a comfort to your kids.

B Join a prayer group at your school, or form one yourself with your friends. Be intentional about keeping prayer a priority. It can be as simple as a texting group.

C Model prayer in all circumstances; prayer in thanksgiving and prayer in times of worries.

D Openly talk to God; this promotes the personal relationship He wants with us.

Suggested Reading and Other Resources

A Bible

B Carol Dweck. *Mindset: The New Psychology of Success*

C Carol Dweck. http://www.edweek.org/ew/articles/2015/09/23/carol-dweck-revisits-the-growth-mindset.html

D Carol Dweck. https://www.ted.com/talks/carol_dweck_the_power_of_believing_that_you_can_improve

E Mark Pett and Gary Rubinstein. The Girl Who Never Makes Mistakes

F JoAnn Deak Ph. D. The Fantastic Elastic Brain: Stretch It, Shape It

G Peter H. Reynolds. The Dot

H Ashley Spires. The Most Magnificent Thing

I Chuck Dervarics and Eileen O'Brien. http://www.centerforpubliceducation.org/Main-Menu/Public-education/Parent-Involvement/Parent-Involvement.html

J Attendance Works. http://www.attendanceworks.org/wordpress/wp-content/uploads/2016/02/Brochure-8.5x11-revised-2016.pdf

K Stephen Manes. <u>Be a Perfect Person in Just Three Days</u>

L https://www.khanacademy.org/

About the Authors

Heather S. Agee received her undergraduate and graduate degrees in education from the University of Florida. Go Gators! She has taught for 12 years in a variety of schools, private, public, and magnet in Virginia, North Carolina, and Florida. She  enjoys partnering with parents to shepherd their children in growing in the knowledge of the Lord.

She is the wife to Jeff for 19 years. They have two children, a 15-year-old son and a 13-year-old daughter. All around Tampa, she if often confused for her identical twin sister. She is a cat-loving and coffee-drinking person and a true follower of Christ.

He tends his flock like a shepherd; He gathers the lambs in his arms and carries them close to his heart; he gently leads those that have young. --Isaiah 40:11

Marie E. Miller received her undergraduate degree from Dordt College and graduate degree from University of Tampa, both in education. She has taught in private schools for 12 years. She loves seeing her students grow closer to the Lord and in their knowledge throughout the year and considers teaching a privilege the Lord has given her.

She also loves spending time with her parents, brothers, and best friend Steph. She adores her two cats and church family.

The path of the righteous is like the morning sun, shining ever brighter till the full light of day. --Proverbs 4: 18

www.ingramcontent.com/pod-product-compliance
Lightning Source LLC
Chambersburg PA
CBHW070630300426
44113CB00010B/1725